DANTE IN CHINA

ALSO BY JOHN BARR

The War Zone

Natural Wonders

The Dial Painters

Centennial Suite

The Hundred Fathom Curve

Grace

The Hundred Fathom Curve: New & Selected Poems

The Adventures of Ibn Opcit

DANTE IN CHINA

poems

John Barr

with an introduction by
Ilya Kaminsky

Red Hen Press | *Pasadena, CA*

Library of Congress Cataloging-in-Publication Data
Names: Barr, John, 1943–author. | Kaminsky, Ilya, 1977–writer of introduction.
Title: Dante in China: new poems / from John Barr; with an introduction by Ilya Kaminsky.
Description: First edition. | Pasadena, CA: Red Hen Press, [2018]
Identifiers: LCCN 2017052823 | ISBN 1597093564 | ISBN 1597090417 |
    ISBN| 1597092509 | eISBN 159709756X
Classification: LCC PS3552.A731837 A6 2018 | DDC 811/.54—dc23
LC record available at https://lccn.loc.gov/2017052823

The National Endowment for the Arts, the Los Angeles County Arts Commission,
the Ahmanson Foundation, the Dwight Stuart Youth Fund, the Max Factor Family
Foundation, the Pasadena Tournament of Roses Foundation, the Pasadena Arts & Culture
Commission and the City of Pasadena Cultural Affairs Division, the City of Los Angeles
Department of Cultural Affairs, the Audrey & Sydney Irmas Charitable Foundation, the
Kinder Morgan Foundation, the Allergan Foundation, the Riordan Foundation, and the
Amazon Literary Partnership partially support Red Hen Press.

First Edition
Published by Red Hen Press
www.redhen.org

GRATITUDE

This book owes a great deal to Ilya Kaminsky and Jim Haines for their advice as fellow poets.

Kate Gale, Mark Cull, and their team at Red Hen make beautiful books. It's an honor to appear in one.

My thanks to the editors of:

Flaunt Magazine, where "Dante in China," "The Nature of Knowing," "Death of a Species," and an excerpt from "Aristotle's Will" previously appeared.

Measure: *A Review of Formal Poetry*, where "Promethean" previously appeared.

War, Literature & the Arts, where "Death of a Species" previously appeared.

Thoreau on Mackinac, where "Oyster House" previously appeared.

"The Book" is for Warren Douglas.

For Blair,
our next generation

CONTENTS

DANTE IN CHINA

INTRODUCTION

1.

At the heart of one's poetics always lies some kind of duality, some kind of contradiction, tension. Yeats's description of it is apt: argument with someone else is rhetoric, argument with oneself is poetry. Yeats, of course, did not invent this: readers of *Hamlet* will notice that the prince is far more likely to speak to others in prose and to himself in verse.

This is not to say that all poets quarrel with themselves in public, in front of us, their readers. But many a poet looks on the things of this world and finds that duality: animals (think of Rilke's panther), objects (think of Neruda's "Ode to My Socks"), historical figures or our very own bodies (much of Cavafy's work), lovers or children (Akhmatova's lyrics), and so on. And anyone who opens this book will find that tension in the very first pages, as John Barr's philosopher-poet addresses a common household plant. ("I am impressed by your tolerance for neglect.") And it is hard not to notice the duality in his description of a bonsai's "exacting balance / of staying alive but only just."

I say the narrator of these poems is a philosopher-poet, but what exactly does that mean? The philosopher speaks of "the importance of suffering," whereas the poet, regarding the bonsai, is quick to find the contradiction in the very first directive we are given, emphasizing to us that "the trick is not to neglect it just enough / but to deny it just enough." The fact that the philosopher's straightforward charge and the poet's slant balancing act appear in the same poem, just a few lines apart (and on many other pages here they appear in the *same* line, often in the same word), points us in the direction of that strange perspective: that of a philosopher-poet, one who inquires into the nature of things while at the same time voicing the very tensions, struggles, and impossible balances of that nature. The philosopher looks to find answers, or warnings, for the questions about our world—but the poet often finds "warnings— / in language he cannot divine." He argues against "the one-wayness of things" and shows us how, despite what we assumed was obvious, "snowfields on the blackest night / [can] be so bright they give back light / that wasn't there." When Dante appears in these pages, it is not in Florence but in China, and he is "stunned / to find Nature so unequivocal."

2.

This book begins with beautiful lyric poems in which the philosopher's outlook is often blended with—and enlarged by—another tonality. Thus, in "Match.com" we get cosmology *and* longing. In "Descant on a Herrick Lyric" we see how Hippocrates' *ars longa, vita brevis* enters the lyric of one of the most famous English erotic poets; their antiphony makes us see "Upon Julia's Clothes" in a slightly different light. Similarly, the wit and bravura of voice in "The Armouress Replies" allow us to see Villon's heroine in a new light, as her response joins eros, humor, and a kind of *ars poetica*. An altogether different kind of knowing is found in the moving poem "Mapping the Interior," where Craig Arnold, a much-missed poet who entered the volcano and never returned, is invoked. As the poet descends, "mapping the interior" like Dante's *Inferno*, we learn what it means "to stay the course—temperature rising toward Absolute Jesus." Here we are met with "burnt chemical flowers of igneous on the boil, / the matter of tomorrow's fire. / A poet's visit, I can tell you, is something strange, / like deputizing the face of chaos." As the poem proceeds, the reader overhears what Craig Arnold comes to know: "The earth we know, / the one we don't: Poetry happens / when it can get its footing properly on neither. // It's the manic in geology that interests me."

This joining of quest for knowledge and mania of the ecstatic (or erotic or mnemonic or audial) instantly appeals as one turns the pages. Thus, in "The Art of the Fugue," we see how the knowledge that comes with age ("for old men, impeccabled by loss, / the lovely alertness of road signs in the Fall / evokes the brotherhood of foxholes") enlarges our sensual appreciation of Bach's late work, and we are led to see how, in the end, "the silence of the room will close / like water without seam." The knowledge is of a different sort in "The Nature of Knowing," where it is gained not through the operation of logic, but from a kind of song, a kind of spell: "Before first light, the first first light— / more night than not— / when what you know is still your own. // In minutes it will be too late, / shape and color / make the strange familiar."

3.

What does this poet-philosopher see in the world around us, how does he go about "deputizing chaos" in our Republic, that is, our late empire that masquerades as "the Republic"? "The known world shrinks to the waters where we sit," he says of "our Republic" where the poet watches "bulldozers / bury our dead while the single-minded calibers / of snipers pick and choose. An officer instructs you / on the animal filth you are: 'Salute. Say Yes.'"

This view is hardly consoling. What consoles is the pleasure of the work, its old-fashioned coupling of wisdom and entertainment, its music as exemplified especially in the long final poem, "Aristotle's Will." To say that this powerfully imagined piece is like nothing in our poetry would be true, but again, what would that mean? For this poem is both historical and fictional—comic, hilarious, deeply ironic and at the same time earnest, heartbreaking, instructive. It is about fathers and sons, teachers and students, arrogance, ignorance, lessons learned, lessons wasted, the indecency of power, the passion, the compassion, the loss. It is a wonderful work.

"As to the exile of the mind there's no such thing"—the poem is filled with such dictums. Listen to this: "Man is an animal. Socrates is a man. / Therefore Socrates is an animal." And this: "How can the beauty of a shoe compare to the beauty of a foot?" These bits of wisdom are coupled with the hilarity of statements such as this one: "The only thing wrong with philosophy: philosophers." There are wonderfully fictional riffs on the private lives of real historical figures who here become memorable—that "gnomelike character, Pythagoras," who like the narrator of this work has "a redeeming sense of humor." As for Socrates, it is hard to refrain from quoting a longer passage:

> The youth of Athens they found to have fallen
>   under the influence of his infectious innocence.
> "Athenians," he asked, "do you offend
>   by policy? Or are you merely oblivious?"
> "Socrates," his friends whispered, "cut the clowning.
>   The point is not to be right but to be alive."
> "I have no opinions," he protested. "Only an attitude problem."
>   As to the last words of Socrates,
>   (who always had to have the last word)
>   accounts differ. According to some:
> "Crito, I owe Asclepius a cock.
>   Will you pay my debt?" To others:
> "Does this mean I won't have to brush my teeth anymore?"
>   But others say he never spoke, never woke.
>   It is said that when the Stygian Cerberus greeted him,
>   Socrates replied: "I won't need
>   an attack dog, thank you. I married one."

As one reads on, it is even harder not to notice how much this narrated world reminds us of our own: "Demagogues are the insects of politics. / Like water beetles they stay afloat / on surface tension; they taxi on iridescence."

This poem's—and the book's—most extended account is also the most moving. It is the story of Alexander of Macedonia, a story of neglect and ambition, anger and (lack of) wisdom, power and the loneliness of a man who thought that "when he makes an empire, he makes a statement," a man who "was good at killing, which he called / 'just plain, unsaturnicated fun.'" It is the story of a man who "with no worlds left to conquer, / wept." It is a story that can be philosophical, funny, and, at the same time, compelling. "One's anger is given to one. The question of achievement is, / what does one turn one's anger into?" In the end it is one of the oldest stories in the world: the choice between wisdom and power, the choice in which "the Philosopher contemplates a road," whereas "the Conqueror is a bad boy with a roadmap." The tragedy of Alexander's empire—and of our contemporary one: "Asked by his generals who would succeed him, / dying Alexander said 'the strongest,' not 'the wisest.'"

In *Aristotle's Will*, Barr's gift as a philosopher-poet is most apparent. We are constantly entertained, we often can't stop laughing out loud, and yet we catch ourselves in the middle of the joke because we are moved by the tragedy—a tragedy that is similar to one that is our own.

—Ilya Kaminsky

LYRIC POEMS

MONSTERA

I know it's in the nature of wonder not to last,
but wonder now at your tactile vigilance,
the quality of attention in this new leaf—
how, learning of light, it unfolds and contorts
in the slow acrobatics of your kind.

I am impressed by your tolerance for neglect.
Latitudes removed from your Latin roots,
you're spared the hazards of the rainforest
if not the usual affronts to household plants—
overwatered or, worse, left waterless.

You're old enough to have followed the neighbor boys
to war and back, but unlike them you self-renew
and never know old age. Had Ponce de León,
when he lay down to die, only known
Eternal Youth bloomed just above his head!

Given modicums of soil, water, air,
new meristems will never cease to grow—
and death for you need never come.
In a world without end you can arabesque,
flourish forever as a species of one.

Which makes my duties for your sustenance
less the chore of an inconstant gardener
than of a monk bringing to the temple
quantities of driest sandalwood
that the fire of fires may never die.

BONSAI MASTER

The trick is not to neglect it just enough
but to deny it just enough.
Decades of managing the stresses
of survival—the exacting balance
of staying alive but only just;
the importance of suffering
to the sublime, against
the inevitable grounds for remorse.

DANTE IN CHINA

Exiled for life, he conceives the Inferno.

Had his wanderings brought him here—*Take Bus 9
for the Red Seabeach*—he might have been stunned
to find Nature so unequivocal.

An endless flat grows nothing normal,
while a weed—arterial red—unrolls
a welcome mat to the unwell.

He sees the tidal river crawl
through deep reversals,
looking for the sea.

He walks the Bridge of Nine Turnings.
Posted up ahead, warnings—
in language he cannot divine.

Strutting cranes patrol
the muck, stab for clams—their shells
like voided efforts at immortality.

Flaring well-gas night and day,
towers rise as if to say,
"Pollution can be beautiful."

He cranes to see what all this will become,
beyond the reach of naked eye,
beyond what earth's receding curve allows.

Sooner or later the bay
will merge with ocean swells,
the only way he can imagine getting home.

MATCH.COM

She's sitting in the breakfast nook
reading the laptop's opened palm;

he's at his desk doing the same,
and fits the profile in her Notebook.

These two are not from ads but real,
and have not found each other because

the sky into which their queries rise
is thick with stars, and even the stars

are only a small part of the spectrum
of the noise of galaxies.

They open like the trumpets of lilies,
like Plato's halves yearning to be whole.

Between them a universe,
only a little of which is visible.

THE ARMOURESS REPLIES

It seemed I heard the one
they called the Armouress
complain, longing for the days
when she was young.
—François Villon, *Le Testament*

My poet-punk, *poète maudit*,
When it comes to women, you know shit.
Look at the girls who've eyes to see
What God gave them for tush and tit:
They set their caps and cruise the street
For some young buck who'll buy them stuff,
Give them a brat at either teat.
They call that home, for them—enough.

Not me. My beauty was of such regard,
Although they called me Armouress
One look at me and men grew hard
To know me by my true name, Amoress.
No Little Lamb but Lioness,
Reclining in a dark-carved gown,
I took it as my pride of place
To reign in the raffish parts of town.

Men of high degree, the higher
Born the better, called on me.
Dressed to the nines in evening attire
Their pants dropped with their dignity.

Even Prelates of the Holy See
Left their angels at the door
To try my Kingdom with their Key.
Like rosary beads, I counted four.

Though I had always honeyness to spare,
My days of coiffed perfection passed.
No longer Countess, not yet whore,
I plied my jaded kittyness
To land the butcher's boy. I took his sass,
The protestations of his love,
His boiled nuts against my ass—
By God, hand never found such glove!

And who would have me now? My Boo-Hoo'd Boy
Gone 30 years, my brief bloom flared to fat,
Behold the glass: my own *memento mori*.
To earn my bread I must submit
To sexual gravel, sexual grit.
(I porter his load, get a grip—
"Old hag, you make love like a vat"—
On all fours make the ancient trip.)

But look at you, Villon. A wine-house spill
Is all it takes to start a fight.
Your rodomontade incites a brawl—

Haymaker left, roundhouse right—
Another larruping, another flight
From roof to roof across *Paree*,
Another pinch, another night
Guest of the Gendarmerie.

You make your bail with a round of rhymes,
Your louche *ballade* a dirty joke:
The Bishop's flustered "Amens . . . ahems!"
As the parish girl of wide-eyed look
Knelt before him and mistook
His proffered finger for the Host,
Then grasped (*here loud guffaws*) his crook:
"For Father, Son, . . . that's not a post!"

But now you've done it. Robbed a church.
Killed a priest. "The last of straws,"
Dehors declares. The jailors birch
Your backside, flay it with the taws.
I seem to hear you sing out your envois
As if any prince would pardon
Such a breaker of the laws,
A pauper-poet and his hard-on.

Item: To Mâitre Villon I'll bring this poem
Where none but the dead would stay to hear,

Some nameless crossroads you call home.
I'll read it through although I fear
You'll have no comment: eyeless, ear-
less, and a raven's got your tongue.
May it coda your career
As the gibbet does the hung.

But who are you to judge, or me?
To profligacy—no tittle no jot unbet—
We gave ourselves. To ardency.
Time tightens and we're both forfeit.
My body's empty as a roadside hut,
Your country of the tongue's a tough terrain.
For you the hangman's tourniquet.
For me the end of just another crone.

DESCANT ON A
HERRICK LYRIC

To say or sing in two voices.

Whenas in silks my Julia goes
Then, then (methinks) how sweetly flows
That liquefaction of her clothes.

Next, when I cast mine eyes and see
That brave vibration each way free
O how that glittering taketh me.

⚬⚬⚬

The merest moment justifies
the labor to perfect the song.
Life is short, art is long.

Exactness captured like a bee
in amber may endure
even to eternity.

⚬⚬⚬

Whenas in silks my Julia goes—
the merest moment justifies—
then, then (methinks) how sweetly flows
the labor to perfect the song,
that liquefaction of her clothes.
Life is short, art is long.

Next, when I cast mine eyes and see
exactness captured like a bee,
that brave vibration each way free
in amber may endure—
O how that glittering taketh me—
even to eternity.

THE ART OF THE FUGUE

The title of Bach's last work,
at the printer when he died.

1.

The left hand iterates, then waits
for the reiterating right.
Then together they expound
in notes both single and in chord,
constructions that exceed
the sum of part and counterpart.

Invention is the word of art.
Whether or not the fugal line,
that cantilevered on its past
never fails to fit
                    off-center with itself,
is in fact invented
or like the statue in the stone
is there already, who can tell?

2.

You do know this. Against entropy,
lost linearities,
the one-wayness of things
a line of notes assays.

With plenties low, food stocks low,
when there is death at birth, the lines
exalt enlargement of the crazed,
anastomose and disembogue.

Despite opinion's angularities,
patronage—or not—of princely states,
the teeter-totter paradox
rejoices in the fitted key.

3.

So does the maple's double clutch
wrest symmetry from earth from air
that its empowered sphere may render
pollen to the wind, then wait.

A great storm sheds the substance of itself
that reservoirs receive, drought recedes.
The new moon waiting for its light discovers,
earth and sun rejoice in syzygy.

How can snowfields on the blackest night
be so bright they give back light
that wasn't there, if not to show
the reach of inward radiance?

For old men, impeccabled by loss,
the lovely alertness of road signs in the Fall
evokes the brotherhood of foxholes.
A siren at dawn, its slow fall
and urgent re-gatherings, recalls
the winnowy thing called song—to sing, sung.
They watch young lovers in the park and see,
athwart the fixed conveyance of the past,
a future opens out . . . antiphonates.
Where once were two there may again be two.

4.

You do know this. After the hands
have worked their figures and stays,
the silence of the room will close
like water without seam. When said and done
the quick decaying notes will leave behind
an unaffected winter afternoon.

Nevertheless they play for us.
The left hand iterates, then waits

THE NATURE OF KNOWING

Ineluctable modality of the visible.

—James Joyce

Before first light, the first first light—
more night than not—
when what you know is still your own.

In minutes it will be too late,
shape and color
make the strange familiar.

An hour from now the sun will flood
the trees with certainties
demanding to be understood.

The agency of objects will insist,
and your life as intuition
for this day will be lost.

THE BOOK

There is no Frigate like a Book
to take us Lands away
—Emily Dickinson

I find you in these sunless stacks.
Your poems might be uncommonly fine—
but your pages darken to brittleness
and you've never been checked out. Unless
your anchor's weighed and you proceed
to find the harbor of another's mind,
nothing will come of the cargo in your hold.
I stand in the gloom of the unread, and read.

MAPPING THE INTERIOR

U.S. professor disappears during Japan volcano hike.
—CNN World, April 30, 2009

Volcanic eruption at Eyjafjallajökull, Iceland
—CNN iReport, April 26, 2010

In April, Craig Arnold entered the volcano.
"Every day poets try to lose control"
(I can hear him say although I never met him)
"in a productive way. The earth we know,
the one we don't: Poetry happens
when it can get its footing properly on neither.

"It's the manic in geology that interests me.
Not the Major Oils whose business is to
find and exploit transsexual oil and gas reserves.
We poets undermine the situate.
It's when energy is nearly not contained—
brio under stress, brisance—
that the human spirit can be rampant.
These are the conditions for grace under pressure.

"Immense, the work, to leave behind the gentled parts,
a lone man loggering, and probe the crags
of the infrastructure skull. Phrenologist's art,
to plumb the fractal welter, enigmatic surfaces
crusted with meaning, and enter the informed

enormity of fastnesses, deeps.
To stay the course—temperature rising toward Absolute Jesus—
down to the anatectic charge in the embers,
burnt chemical flowers of igneous on the boil,
the matter of tomorrow's fire.
A poet's visit, I can tell you, is something strange,
like deputizing the face of chaos."

April to April he traveled through the earth
exiting the eruption at Eyjafjallajökull.
"Living or dead we add no weight to the dead weight
of a trundling planet. Our spark weighs naught as a neutrino
but is the imperiled particle of Original Resolve."

2012: a record year for solar storms.
Craig has his eye on those as well,
the hydrogen fire, bright button of awarded sun.

DEATH OF A SPECIES

> *The earth doesn't need to be saved. . . . 99 percent of*
> *all species have come and gone while the planet has*
> *remained.*
> —Lilienfeld and Rathje

The long republic shells the long republic
of itself. Large-minded calibers
open in front of us. Of their swell and pass
Hemingway observes, "The one that fucks you
you won't hear." Orwell muses,
". . . not so much afraid of being hit

but that you don't know *where* you will be hit."
Staggered by airstrikes, our remaindered Republic
falls to an endless enfilade. Bulldozers
bury our dead while the single-minded calibers
of snipers pick and choose. An officer instructs you
on the animal filth you are: "Salute. Say Yes."

The brown sausage of your tongue, the boils and pus,
the Copacabana in your gut that gives you the shits
are gifts of the tiny goddess that infects you.
Despite the frantic scrubbings with carbolic
the life boils out of you. The plague ship sails—cadavers
for cargo, us for crew—on the ultimate in cruises.

We never expected rains, let alone the sluices
of Heaven. The sea's rise the land's loss,

the last of the surf-encircled summits disappears.
The known world shrinks to the waters where we sit,
fathoms above the topsoils of our Republic—
or, given the lack of landfalls, maybe Timbuktu.

Watching the rivers freeze, the glaciers grow, what strikes you
is, there *is* a Hell and this is how it freezes.
Knapped point hafted, held on a throwing stick,
we follow the herd that opens the snow in search of grass.
In the Great Depopulation birth rates plummet,
feeding chains collapse. Our species takes a number.

The moon's not right—the side-lit lavender sphere careers.
What are the odds a button of neutron star strikes through
our mere-most crust, taking a piece of planet with it?
The earth unbelts from orbit. Losing light and gases
it seeks a farther place in time and space.
Etiolate . . . hypoxic . . . and now we are relict.

And now you can declare it. Calibers
or spears, king or republic, what finally fucks you—
take it from the Muses—is: *This too shall pass.*

OYSTER HOUSE

Blue Point, Skookum, Kumamoto—
Malpeque!

In rings of a dozen they arrive;
each shell enthrones a puddled king.
Sitting with us, pitching in,
the hoplite scarfs his *ostrean*,
the lictor wolfs his *ostrea*,
the Breton gargles his *huîtres*.
All downed with a chalky, cheerful Chablis.

The piles of shells go out to the dumpster—
buttonized for jewelry,
pulverized for roadbed by the ton.

And what of you, Filter Feeders?
How do you answer the reavers—
waterman, starfish, gull—
out of deep time?

Let just one of you, turned female,
release 100 million eggs:
the tide dims, spat settle,
whole reefs rise
from your animal magnitude.

And why else would the whelk
lift secretion to an art form,
if not for immortality?

ARISTOTLE'S WILL

ARISTOTLE'S WILL

Prologue

"Until philosophers rule as kings or kings truly philosophize, cities will have no rest from evils. Until power and philosophy coincide, there will be no happiness for the human race." So Plato described the ideal ruler of his Republic. But Aristotle, pupil of Plato and tutor to Alexander, saw better than any the philosopher and king at their extremes, and questions if there can ever be a Philosopher King.

I. EXILE

In lateral cascades the sea arrives, arrives
to thunder on the shoreline of Euboea.
If Empedocles was right, that the elements are borne
of loathings and affinities, are we to think
the loathing of fire for water, its ardency for air,
the loves of salt for water and water for earth converged
upon the gritty undersubstance of the void
to give us this template of the world called Greece?
I watch the relentless pour of the Aegean and think
water can turn to water almost anything.

Plato had it wrong. The *idea* of a house
is not a house. A house is an assemblage of planks
where I, Aristotle—familiar and philosopher
to kings—can study the manly arts of keeping house.
A regular Betsy Neat and Clean, I build the fire,
try to warm the place without burning it down,
attend the pleasures of the hearth: the bustle
of boiling water, a coney's loin, a little meat for the mind.
Very little. How often do worthwhile thoughts arise
in the deeps of night when a victim of inslumbia
shuffles the house in piss-cankered sandals?
Or at first light, when the nightingale clears its throat?
The logs slip and settle: The fire studies
how to survive without the help of Aristotle.

As to the exile of the mind there's no such thing.
Athens, I knew it when it was a place Macedonians
went to be sick after drinking. It still is.
Ask Socrates, who said to the Athenians
as he quaffed his dram of unmitigated gall,
"Is truth-telling always an act of self-destruction?"
Ask Plato, who scorned their plebiscite conspiracies
and died sadder if not wiser. When Alexander,
dead of conniption in a foreign land,
no longer rode the agora in celebrated bronze,
that there would be hell to pay was clear. I gave them
no second chance to sin against philosophy.

So here am I, escaped with my mortality.
No longer to visit my beloved bestiary,
down past the pestularium and breeding ring
to the fragrant pens with their douzaine of oddities:
The Dromedary of a single hump. The pig
as Pygmy Elephand. The Greater Elephand
that moves with the surpassing slowness of the Dinnosaur.
The Hyptorax, an animal that backs up poorly
but drags cargo with its teeth. The Gryphon,
for whom flight is but heavy flapping.
The advantaged Phoenix, whose presence
with us is a blessing without context.
And of course my legendary Unicorn.

(That this stallion of a single horn comes
from a marriage of horse and crystal, who can doubt?)
No more to wander those compounds of original wonder,
now stables of the dead, dying, or escaped.

Nor is the Lyceum any longer mine to lead.
My students would ask, in the subservient sedate,
and I would teach the Aristotelian mind-grinder
of the day, going to and fro and up and down
the shady walks. Thus did they pay attention for stadia.
Accused of the reckless endangerment of ingénieux,
Aristotle is forbidden to lead the young
to the awful dawning of intelligence. No more,
the mighty syllogism as my cantilever,
to build out, on the known, great superstructures
of supposition: *We take this to be apodictic.*
Man is an animal. Socrates is a man.
Therefore Socrates is an animal. No more
to carry it forward, even though it settles nothing.

I have my writings: the work of a life of 60 years,
to all things an answering, surmounting mind.
"Thousands of pages of dyspepsia," some say,
"distinctions passing for intelligence."
"My job," I answer, "is to organize
the Cosmos, not to make it entertaining."

For the true benefit of writing is to produce
not action or even understanding, but the peace
of mind that comes with the act of articulation.

And you, Mediocrates, will take notes faithfully
as if (Heaven forefend) they were the only record
to survive of Aristotle's final thoughts, last licks.
For you are the Drat Boy, whose job it is to serve your betters
while they tell you about your illicit parentage.

II. PLATO'S WILL

We live in a jokeless time. In Athens now there are
no clowns and little chance of honesty.
But 40 years ago it was the only home
to that enthralled milieu they call philosophy.
It was the place where young men, walking abroad
with minds like countries without borders, ended up.
The place where wannabe philosophers—
the protuberant anybodies of their class—
could hope to add to the weight of wisdom already enscrolled.
But Athens then was not a place, it was a state of mind.
Philosophy should be a timeless enterprise,
where spirit and idea converge, congrue;
where high concerns of state and soul can be discussed
in reasoned, ecumenical debate.
So philosophy should be. But in Athens
it was a contact sport. A blood sport.

The only thing wrong with philosophy: philosophers.
They sit around posing effete questions
to one another, with elaborate courtesies
confound each other's minds. "How can the beauty
of a shoe compare to the beauty of a foot?"
They founded schools for the untoward and incapable.
Enrolling young men whose minds are clean of instruction,
they put them through logical hell; in the imperious
prerogative demand, "What is the rule that these

exceptions prove?" Disdimnified, their students shrug:
"We wouldn't know where to find the answer for *that*."

The worst of the philosophes were the arrivistes
who arrove each month to make their reputation.
Entering a salon like a saloon they would demand,
"So what's the standard of perfection around here?"
They pushed cantankerous to a malign metaphysics.
Crappus, who held that man is too good to be great.
Antithesis, who countered, "Man, it's good to be great."
They would get mad about unusual things. Philander,
who apologized for the letter F. ("All my values
are words starting with A through E.") Meander,
that master of logic's undeviating line. Anopheles
and his incorrigible pal Juris Prudence:
two failed philosophes from the city of Minutia,
hoping to become the world's first law firm.
"For law is reason without desire. Justice is with.
Besides," they said, "we find humor in arraignments."

The oddest of the lot were the first scientists.
Terras Firmas maintained the earth was a breaded ball.
(For that eruptive nonsense he was properly hanged.)
Emulctiphei of Phlogiston proclaimed the world
made of zircon, hornblende, biotite, and feldspar.
"Not so," said Nemesis. "Bismuth, porphyry,

antimony, and swamp gas." The worst was Democritus
who claimed matter to be made of atoms.
On the face of it, ridiculous. How
could the little spheres cohere? Our life
would be all slipping and sliding. (*Possibly*
it's made of little cubes.) But he couldn't stop there.
"All energy is waves. Quick then,
how many million photons in the room just now?"
(He was excitable, at least at the electron level.)
"I see," I said. "So sound is a low form of light,
our ears are eyes, and what we hear we see?" Really.

But few could hold a candle to Pythagoras,
who billed himself "the Father of Mathematica."
A gnomelike character, Pythagoras
had a dolichocephalic head.
It came that way, willi-wakka out of the womb.
(Isosceles, his student, had one shaped like a triangle.)
Precocious and crazed, by the age of three
he could count by multiples of 23.
Equations he solved in his head as parlor tricks:
"The answer, one hundred divided by two, backed by seven."
He played lavish mathematical jokes on his friends:
"Take this number, square it, and shove it up your numerator."
He gave geometry its founding principles:
    ♦ *A point is the beginning of a straight line.*

- *A spiral is a circle made by the drunken driving of that point.*
- *A cylinder? An O driven through space.*
- *As the radius of a circle has one foot nailed
   and drags the other for circumference,
   so it does a backflip for diameter.*

Lesser known is that Pythagoras
worked out his theorems with the aid
of his concubine Numerica. She loved
to subtend the arc of his regard,
to play the lowest common denominator.
He entered her as 3 goes into 2, unevenly.
By her he had his daughter Mathematica.
Grown old he died of a heart attack. "Oh my God,
I think I'm having an integer."

But even Pythagoras could not match Socrates.
The first thing you noticed, he was a bit inane.
Never a revel but his pug-dog face
and inestimable paunch showed up
like an uninvited consequence.
Watching him settle down to a long *Issatzo* night
you saw that for him arguing was a sign of respect.
He deplored dismissive ambiguity;
his true occupation was exactitude.
He could spend an evening on the difference
between ubiquitous and omnipresent,

between meticulous and fastidious.
That's how good he was. And how irrelevant.
It was his habit, distracting and intractable,
to prove his students definitionally inconstant.
He turned his knack for that into a mastery.
He had a redeeming sense of humor. (But then
a sense of humor can redeem most anything.)
The convivial intellectual establishment
of Athens found *him* to be guilty of malapropism.
The youth of Athens they found to have fallen
under the influence of his infectious innocence.
"Athenians," he asked, "do you offend
by policy? Or are you merely oblivious?"
"Socrates," his friends whispered, "cut the clowning.
The point is not to be right but to be alive."
"I have no opinions," he protested. "Only an attitude problem."
As to the last words of Socrates,
(who always had to have the last word)
accounts differ. According to some:
"Crito, I owe Asclepius a cock.
Will you pay my debt?" To others:
"Does this mean I don't have to brush my teeth anymore?"
But others say he never spoke, never woke.
It is said that when the Stygian Cerberus greeted him,
Socrates replied, "I won't need
an attack dog, thank you. I married one."

Which brings me to Plato. I remember him
an aristocracy of one, high-born
of the cared-for enclaves; a citizen
of the world equally at ease
with idolatries of muscle at the Games
or the protocols of speakeasies
or studies of the abstruse and occult.
Under the sway of Socrates, his study
was of the minds of his time, the rival philosophes.
But those masters of the lorgnette universe
gave him only lozenges of knowledge,
an exhaustion of old theologies.
He said to me, "I have that restlessness
a snake must feel before it molts. I must
look beyond the many for the One."
Roaming the arroyos of his mind,
the locked canyons of his dreams, he asked,
"How many layers *does* reality have?"
After months of this miasmic enterprise
I saw him again and was astounded:
the tortured portal of his face, the shell
of a man haunted from the inside out.
He had just written *The Republic*.

If the perfect is the enemy of the good,
The Republic is the enemy of human nature.

His prescription for the perfect state
was *not* democracy. "The rule of the mob
is what killed my Socrates and, worse,
democracy mutates into despotism."

He despises demagogues, "who use
the frenzy of the jawbone to arouse
the hatred of the Have-Nots for the Haves.
Demagogues are the insects of politics.
Like water beetles they stay afloat
on surface tension; they taxi on iridescence."

And he hates the despots demagogues become.
"Through the management of chaos they align
the people, march them to the awarded tempo
until it is the death of custom, end of wonder.
Out of his subjects the tyrant teases—with chain fall
and sledge—compliance and respect,
loyalty expressioned in the taken oath."

And he rejects the kings of old, "who taught
our task, no matter what, is to obey.
All of them claimed divine authority
as they played their ancient games of Rot & Throw.

"Only a King who is also a Philosophe,
whose wisdom reasons with his power,
can rule with justice in my perfect State."
That was Plato's Republic, and it nearly
got him killed.

          Dion, Plato's friend,
invited him to the Kingdom of Syracuse,
there to establish his Republic "in the flesh."
"Tutor my royal charge, Dionysius,
who has acceded to his father's throne.
Make of him the first Philosopher King!"

Clueless Plato sailed to Syracuse
and set up shop. But when the callow King,
who was something of a party animal,
heard Plato say that he would have to lead
a Spartan life, he asked, "How's that again?"
And when he heard his royal powers would be shared
among some group of strangers called the "Guardians"
he called "Time Out." And when he learned
the women would be shared and shared alike
as common property, he drew the line.
At this point the sycophants and *Party On*!
companions of his Nibships went to work.
"Quisling Dion," they whispered, "joins with Plato;
they conspire to upend your Kingdom.

You and your retinue—that would be us—
are to be exiled to a desert isle
yet to be determined." The whispers did their work.
Blameless Dion found himself banished
and Plato, impounded, was sold into slavery.
Displayed in stocks in the agora, he was hung with a sign
"Philosopher King—Get Your Wisdom Here."
Pelted with garbage, begrimed with shit and dungeon straw,
poor Plato was ransomed and returned to Athens,
on his back the stripes of the world not as it should be,
but as it is. Thus ended Plato's first and only Republic.

III. ALEXANDER'S WILL

I was summoned by Philip of Macedon,
father of Alexander the yet-to-be-Great.
His Court lies in the ancient capitol of Pella,
a place where things ride into town and fall apart.
For 300 years they have been perfecting snobbery,
the citizens raising unwelcome to an art form.
I found two courtiers, giggling at the sort of thing
that is extremely funny but cannot be shared.
Asked the Royal whereabouts, they chortled and buttoned up.
"Goddab the goddab dab the goddab dab!"
From a full city block, a voice was reckoning.
I found Philip emerging from the Imperial waste barge,
muttering, "Cobfounded 'traption, I hate what you stand for!"
"Is there a problem, your Majesty?" I asked.
"Whed I swallow, my ears, which are filled with phleb, cauldron."
He swallowed, which broke up assemblages of phlegm
in the back of the Royal throat. He coughed up a crème brûlée.
Expertly he hawked the lunger for the far side.
"And how's the knee?" I asked of his wound. "Buch better, thag you."
And off he hobbled with an energetic humping of the elbows.

Philip was broke just then, but wanted me to tutor Alex.
With a *How-much-is-this-going-to-cost-me?* look, he spoke:
"We give you the clean surface of his mind on which to write.
Teach him the time-honored ways to get away with murder.
If you're a King, crime pays. So does petulance.

But there is a parade ground of knowledge that goes with that.
The man who would be King must also be a Philosophe.
Tell him that when he makes an empire, he makes a statement
about what he stands for, who he is. Place my son
where the lives of action and of contemplation converge."
Then Alex, in the tubular shorts of the very young,
ran in like a scare of teeth. His one word he practiced
with the repetition of an oarlock: "Conquer! Conquer! Conquer!"
Of little Alex I may say he did not suffer
from an indiscriminate need to please. Quickly
he decided I was a numma-gumma No Fun;
he wouldn't play. Philip, flexing his Mercy Cane,
said, "You know children. Awful by policy."
Then proceeded to beat him pretty much into submission.
"I hope I didn't create a monster. But I am
getting old and maybe not as flexible
as I never was. See what *you* can do."
Those years of tutoring the wildness
of Alexander, of playing the indulgent uncle!
Neutered pigs, stoned sheep, poisoned wells—
he dined on a repast of vandalism,
after which he seemed to feel a measure of peace.
I truckled to his snapdammits of incomprehension,
sought to teach him *noblesse oblige*, the fame of virtue
vs. the fame of authority. ("Do I *have* to choose?")
"Alex," I asked, "is it easier to change the world

or change your mind?" Alex answered, "Ari,
I love it when you talk dirty to me about *akrasia.*"
Understand, Aristotle's will was nothing
as to Alexander's: "You wish me to study, to accumulate
as much knowledge as possible," he said. "Instead,
I expect to retain only what I need."
I assigned him, already at the sharp art of war
better than any, "The Views of Military Commanders
on Pillaging, Raping, and Looting." He chose to write, instead,
an essay on "The Philosophe as Bullshit Artist."
Only once did Philip call me in, when Alex showed
a passing interest in painting. "We find it inappropriate,
this flicker of talent in the Royal line."

The death of the father is important as it dates the son.
And one man's circle of friends is another's cabal.
After the blow, the back of Philip's head was *repoussé*;
the anlace, like a boundary stake, stood upright in his back.
When the King was buried, a waxen effigy, in his barrow,
and the fires of succession were burning high and anxious,
I looked for Alex of the barely emergent beard.
I found him in the stables watching a red-hot horseshoe,
how the *soft* of the iron listened to the smithy's hammer.
"I thought I might have had the chance to stand for something."
For the one time in his life I saw his swallowing
mechanism break down. He cried, and I saw

the doors of childhood swing open onto wilderness.
"As a son to his father is the emissary seed
 was I to Philip, a portable version of himself."
"Alex, that a person should be formed
 and settled by 17, that is unusual.
 And in your case, out of the question.
 Cheated of a father who would tell you you were good,
 you are a young man trying to be a dynasty."
"There is a past and it's worth preserving," he replied.
"There is a future and it's worth preserving, too."
 When I urged him to accept a regent, Alex
 answered, "The world will not hold still so long."
 And thus was born the Alexandriat.

One's anger is given to one. The question of achievement is,
what does one turn one's anger into? Alexander
gave the Court no chance to adopt him, to entrap him
in the schemes of the great houses of the town.
He made known the Here and Now of his intent.
He earlied his plans to lay the heuristic stone.
He summoned the army. They came like moths
to a torch's billowing flame, to the magnet and mystery
that lives as potential in the human soul.
To a man they acted under the influence of his will.
He drilled them to move—*Hit—Hight—Hat—Hut—*
like his pride and purpose, of a piece.

Trained to a T they moved with rambunctious symmetry,
phalanx for defense, cavalry for attack.
At the head of the enameled shells of his chariots
rode this fine figure of a swath-cut man;
rode, to the musical thunder, Alexander. And all of them
learned the business of the flag is never done.

He challenged them first to the trial by Greek.
The zealous overbite of Macedonia
he applied to the rebellious Thracians,
defiant Thebans, petulant Athenians.
His army swallowed the Greek peninsula entire.
Caught in the swing and fest of victory, he asked,
"What's next?" Alex yearned for Asia, long sought long since,
like an unfinished piece of his father's business,
like an extended form of self-knowledge.
Uncertain only of his own impatience, he said:
"Vast Asia I would not embrace without a sign.
Aristotle, go consult the oracles:
Shall I forge forward in the holy hope of empire?"

Now it is my plain, ungumpered view that the future,
generally, is not to be trusted. That the views of those
who claim to be informed by a knowledge of what comes next
are as interesting and useful as a lock without a key.
But dutifully I sought them out, starting with

Yarbo the Entirely Manic, an accomplice of Esto
the Maniac and his farmer-brother Isto the Manioc.
These soothsayers took their bearings from the moon
(which for me is but an exact, pockmarked record
of itself). Masters of the catatonic fit,
they wouldn't leave it alone.
"This is Bedullah. This is what she says:
Beware of worry, of warnings, of advisories."
"But what sign should we watch for, what signal see?" I asked.
"Boil the heart of a hecatombed ox and you will hear
the heart-song of the god." "This matter of looking at entrails,"
I said, "and not being very good at it:
Is it a silliness at which we all can play?"
When I suggested they come clean, they said,
"We don't know. Tell him it's way too early to be lucky."

Next I tried diviners skilled in the arts
of glossolalia, echolalia, ululation.
Moonmoth and Monsong: Of this *ensemble dedouble*
I chose the better of the lesser of the two.
By an eye trick from the insect world,
Moonmoth was way to the left of weird. He spoke
with the confidence of one who counts on being misunderstood.
(Just once I'd like to hear a soothsayer try
to explain himself, to make himself clear.)
"A combination of joy and urgency

the Hurry Up of Hush and Rush fit together
in the way they were meant to fit, and not."
"And where, oh fell, swooney spirit, does that leave me?"
"That was the sacred part. Wait till you hear the profane."
"Don't be nonsense-ridiculous. I could do better
with a fortune cookie than talking
to fart-tongued oracles like you."
He shrugged and said, "Join us at the pig sear."

The best I saved for last: the Delphic Oracle.
"Do you have an account with us? Do we have you on file?"
their spokesman asked. "For we too are touched,
stroked by the fingers of economic need."
The Oracle, who uses live chickens for pillows,
divines by having a fit. In a hairdo of death,
she inhales a bubbling barley of unnamed drugs,
she sweats, she breaks into warts. "What will be,"
she groaned, "different from what was . . ." "The principal value
of the study of history," I had to interject,
"is to teach us that things need not be as they have been . . ."
"SILENCE!" There was silence. "Tell Alexander
the cornucopia starts to feed on itself."
Then, her face like a slice of chaos, she started on me.
(Why, of the years of Aristotle's century,
did she count backward from 400?
And who is this carpenter? And where is Galilee?)

Whatever the strange evasion ropes by which they work,
the task of oracles, I believe, is to know
not the future but their client's mind,
and to help him on his way.

                        Alexander went straight
for Persia, the unsanctified heart of Hither Asia.
Pausing only at the Hellespont while his oracles
made sacrifice, a blue haze at a time, he crossed
and won a purchase on the shores of excitable light.
He didn't have long to wait. His troops in wonder watched
the approach of Persian armies numbered in the scads.
At night their fires were as the stars
come down on the hills to camp. And in their midst
was Darius, King of Persia, King of Kings.
Alexander sued for parley and approached.
On oriental carpets of the Early Despots period
sat the fabulous potentate, like a hill upon a hill.
Pedicured, in his crust of jewels reptilian,
sat this enormous *grunsagh* of a man.
And atop this imperial avalanche,
like a hill upon a hill upon a hill,
perched the shaved head and globular lips of Darius.

"Hi," said Alexander. "Your name must be Corpus."
"So this is the stripling waiting for applause,"

said Darius, "who must be the talk of everybody's town.
We have heard of your victories. Like a dog farting in Greece."
"I thought I was doing nicely if not well.
But I'm about to regret coming here, aren't I.
I suppose it's too late to stop? To just turn in my ATTACK button?"
"Yours is a presence that lacklusters my lands.
So we are going to manifest your destiny.
First we're going to give you an embolism on the spot.
Then we're going to send your head on a world tour.
The rest of you we'll make a steaming pile
of breakfast offal to which my dogs will help themselves.
Have you seen my Borborygmus bolt his food?
He has a mouth like a dormer window. Like a coal chute.
His throat is but the entrance to his anus.
You'll be famous all right. For being dead."
To this Alexander listened like a foregone conclusion.
"I'm sure all that is true, even if only a little.
But better to move over than to leave,
I always say. Your Amenhotepships,
nothing has a right to the space it occupies."

Returned, Alexander addressed his troops.
He had learned not how to project his voice,
but how to hurl it. As he exhorted from
a portable vaunt, I watched his animated back.
"We had a meaningful five minutes of conversation.

I would describe the exchange as frank and businesslike.
Oh he gave a pretty good explanation of certain consequences;
he showed the extent to which threats can be understated
and still effective. But the man is void of enthusiasms.
He has no vision of what's new and could be next.
It's tyrants like him that give my calling the name it has.
These Persians lack the force of their own evil."
Asked how the Greeks, in thousands 30 to the 600
of Darius, could possibly hope to prevail, he said,
"Because my anger is bigger than his anger.
One thing I trust in is my anger:
I take umbrage easily. In Darius
I see a man in the business of tending
his reputation—in his case a full-time job.
I see a man turning into curlicues,
an ornament, a Not Much Else.
While they rhetoric the royal We
and meet on precedent, we'll be terriers."
Then Alexander spoke the words that entered history:
"We're going to tear the man a new asshole."

Not one to observe from a hill his armies clot and collide,
not one to watch his wounded wobble off to die,
Alexander in battle became alive in another way.
Grabbing his killing gear he leapt aboard
that unsaddled euphoria Bucephalus,

horse of 18 hands that he alone could tame.
Always he sought the center of the fray.
Ever he assumed the greater risk.
Singing a goresong, he cried "Bitch." And "Botch."
And "Watch out, Rubber Nose." Craving an opponent
he would pick one out and pick him out right now.
With hard things they scored each other;
they tried for bone-on-bone conclusions.
The blunt trauma of a mace, swung to make
of Alexander's mouth a bloody chow,
he ducked and thrust beneath the hoplite's iron hide.
"You took my pancreas!" his enemy cried
and crashed like an oak tree, vomiting blood.
Alex was good at killing, which he called
"just plain, unsaturnicated fun."

The end of that great battle on the Persian plain
found Alexander still standing. His mail
was deconstructed—his body bled through sushi wounds—
and well he knew the metallic taste of blood.
But around his head he wore a crown of domain dust.
"Well," he said, surrounded by all the dead that ever were,
"at least we've taken care of the population pressure."
He bent over a corpse; he closed the eyes. He shook his head;
he opened them. "One thing about carrion,"
he said, "you don't have to get personal with it."

Then he turned to face the humongous interlude
of Asia. By the seamless segue of road to road,
the squiggles of his armies moving inland
practiced the time-honored art of barn-burning,
the left and right of pillaging and laying waste.
Like herds before a lion the peoples of Asia ran
before him in a sheer of terror; like gazelle
hoping in the safety of numbers not to get picked.
Some understood that freedom's not worth dying for.
They shrugged. They surrendered. And Alexander said,
"Let there be enfilial tarnhausen between us."
Of these he said, "You don't kill 'em. You convert 'em.
It's a matter of paying the light tribute due."
They genuflected; they gave him enacted submission.

But some, like the city of Tyre, paved the roads
with goofing tiles and swore to the last man to resist.
Following his father's dictum ("First beseech, then besiege.")
Alexander stood before the smooth walls climbing
out of sight and issued his fearsome behest.
They laughed (*Ahafne Ahafne Geroot Geroot*)
and called down, "Look who's calling who a barbarian."
Then Alexander unlimbered his husky engines of siege:
The Bombast and the Bombard and the Knock Down such
that no tenon in no toehold mortise could withstand.
The entire city of Tyre a collapsing salute,

their side became the fallen side. Said Alex,
"I know it's priceless cultural artifacts," kicking
the ruins into a ruckus of sparks, "but this is business."
The men he butchered, the women and children he sold as slaves.
He learned to deal with enemies through the broken word.
He sponsored novel conspiracies. To traitors
he gave enormous, arm-damaging gratuities.
Potentates with names like interjections—
Bedevil Himsavil, Yars Tattibus, Havarté Gongol,
the Brutal ("Welcome to Ulan Bator") Anglliermo,
the Fissiparous Barbooth (who, eating his blood pudding,
was willing to call a spade a spade), even
the Tempestuous Khan—all came to call him "Boss."

From the ranges of the Coohatchee to the upper reaches
of the Artvong; from the bare bones of the Yamma Yen
to the wide and sideways kingdom of Güsh;
from the flatlands of the peoples of the Oven Grass
to the cloven fractals of the Himalays:
at the midwinter gathering known as the *stampersyong*
Alexander was offered the double palm of Afganijuice.
He sat to the feast of baboon in its lacquer of salt,
to mounds of crustaceans boiled and cashiered of shell.
Leg and leg he straddled the fabulated dotted line
that severs Wednesday from Tuesday, the seam of time
that makes things right, known as the Chaldean Date Line.

It was Wednesday. It was Tuesday.
It was Asia. It was Greece. It was Alexander.
In his wake he left a string of sequacious satraps
(The Demiurge O'Datawa; the Egad of O'Deffadad).
His grasp on faraway, breakaway cities was *sans pareil*.
His strategy: to be present by being absent.
His Court, full of novitiate snobs, he used to create
communal subservience and a good deal of stress.
"We want sound men," he said, "of sibilance and no substance.
Of pinched goatee and feckless vest,
egg on their robes and molder in their hair."

They say that Alexander, with no worlds left to conquer,
wept. I wouldn't know. There is this urge
in men to go where they are most alive.
For Alex that was combat, hand-to-hand,
the settlement of things by sword and spear.
But the end of the violence from without left nothing
for the violence within to push against.
That left, as next best thing, debauchery.
With his generals—all of them crazy as loons, as coots—
he tied on royal bender after royal bender.
Bowls of unmixed wine, beers by the double quaff
produced an acceptable *riage*. Once in his cups
Alexander could be jolly, quite irresistible.
It could be a series of yoking jokes with his dwarf—

a man of tragic height who drolled for a living—
or with me, whose job it was to distract
the Monarch from his megalomania.
("I'd like to thank my friend Ari
for alerting me to that particular peccadillo.")
But he could darken sudden as a thunderstorm.
Then his guests, fearing a spear, crawled under tables.

One night I woke to a sound outside my tent:
The robust noise of piss filling a bucket.
Alex entered, his great cape wrapped against the cold,
and sat on my bed. He was encrusted with exhaustion.
"I have been wondering if I am not a god.
But for the needs for food and generation"
(not his exact words) "I would forget
that I am not a god." "Your Majesty," I said,
"can you be *in* the world if not *of* it?"
"Achilles was. Born of a goddess. And I
am descended from Achilles. The question matters
because I cannot face the sin of growing old.
Can you imagine Achilles old? I cannot.
Will it be my fate to sit the peacock throne
playing the Persians against the Phrygians
against the Parthians, giving what monarchs give,
denying what they always deny?
Will I recede into petulant renown,

the fabulous gold placidity of Darius?
Aged, will I be a fat thing full of air,
of frets and frailness, body parts letting go,
ending in a greatest-ever funeral pyre?"
He raised his empty tankard. "You're missing the party."

When does inanity become insanity?
His benders went from time to time, to all the time.
He swore an oath against sobriety.
When he threw up, with hearty dammits he unmoored
his dinner from the stomach's hold.
Flensed with sweat he disgorged all he knew
of tenderloin, the spring potatoes, leek soup.
He withheld nothing until at last he pumped
an empty bellows, a few humors, an All Souls belch.
Court he held above the crapper's golden rim.

One morning he awoke, dry with the killing dry
of alcohol. He drained a double flagon.
"One for me, one for the Sea Monster in my head."
A wide smile breached his face. "Nothing to see here, folks."
Then he died in place.

Of this king of kings what is there to say?
For some: "Well, there's another myth disbanded."
For some: "He showed how inefficient travel is."

And some: "In a business known for hubris, he stood out."
But Aristotle says that Alexander showed
that things don't have to be the way they are.
Men change begrudgingly. They say,
"Whatever happens, happens again." But Alexander
showed a new order is there for the imagining.
And those who do not invent the future will have to endure it.
To the Asia that would not, he said,
"Whatever works. Whatever I can take by will."
Alexander climbed the summit of the world.
"And so I said. And so I did." And so was Great.

IV. ARISTOTLE'S TESTAMENT

All civilization starts with a cooking fire.
The Philosopher considers the nature of that fire,
how it subsumes whatever wood is
to whatever flame is.
The Conqueror will use that fire to set more fires.

The Philosopher contemplates a road,
how it wants to curve the same way every day.
The Conqueror is a bad boy with a roadmap.
He takes the fast roads out of town.

The Philosopher asks, "What is a bird without wings?
A species of feathered rat." The King, his armies
in battle order, watches the birds for auguries.
He sees the heron standing like a stilt,
hears crows, propounding territory, caw.
Then: a sudden black flapping of wings.

The Philosopher marvels at how the galleys
put to sea as if spoken by the harbor's mouth.
For the Conqueror the deep engagements
of the oars are fulcrums whose labors
move the ocean to move the earth.

Plato, who would get to the bottom of everything,
believed too much the smolderings in his head.

How *could* he, the ultimate man of the mind,
come up with a State on its face so ridiculous?
"Notion sickness" is what I say of his Republic.

Alexander was wary of thinkers. "Conquest
is an animal enterprise, the stuff of Ulysses,
hardly the business of philosophes.
It takes not wisdom but impatience—will
and willfulness. Ambition is my burning bush."
Asked by his generals who would succeed him,
dying Alexander said, "the strongest,"
not "the wisest." Alex was all Achilles.

Shall the world be conquered by mind or muscle?
In the realm of action Plato failed.
In contemplation Alexander failed.
If even these could not encompass both,
then mind and muscle will contend
even to the end of things, and never
come to terms in a Philosopher King.

But character is what determines fate,
with or without the guiding hands of gods.
And character is conduct carried out
long after circumstances warrant,

condemn, condone, or even honor it.
It's the wealth or poverty of any state.

Above the windy Aegean, here
at house's prow I write my testament.
I have lived fully and well. It remains to die well.
(The fully takes care of itself.) It is Aristotle's will.

NOTES

"Monstera" (Page 9)
In Zoroastrian temples the daily offering of sandalwood to a consecrated fire is an act of veneration.

"Dante in China" (Cover and Page 12)
The largest reed marsh in the world, the Red Seabeach in Panjin, China, is so alkaline that nothing will grow but a seepweed that turns bright red in autumn.

"The Armouress Replies" (Page 15)
La Belle Heaulmière (the Helmetmaker's Wife) was, in her day, a famous beauty and demimondaine. Villon would have known her as she appears in Rodin's sculpture *The Old Courtesan.*
Pierre de la Dehors was Villon's jailer.

"Mapping the Interior" (Page 26)
Eyjafjallajökull: AY-uh-fyat-luh-YOE-kuutl-uh

BIOGRAPHICAL NOTE

Over the past 30 years John Barr's poems have been published in two books by Red Hen Press (*The Hundred Fathom Curve: New & Collected Poems* and *The Adventures of Ibn Opcit*, a two-volume mock epic); two books by Story Line Press (*The Hundred Fathom Curve* and *Grace*); and four hand-printed editions by Warwick Press (*The War Zone, Natural Wonders, The Dial Painters,* and *Centennial Suite*).

Barr was born in Omaha in 1943 and grew up in a rural township outside of Chicago. A graduate of Harvard College and Harvard Business School, he served five years as a Navy officer, which included three tours to Vietnam. In a 30-year career as an investment banker he was managing director at Morgan Stanley and founded three start-ups. He has taught in the Graduate Writing Program at Sarah Lawrence College and served on the boards of Yaddo, Bennington College, and the Poetry Society of America, the latter two as board chair. In 2004 he was appointed inaugural president of the Poetry Foundation and served in that capacity for its first decade.